My Spine

by Rena Korb

illustrated by Rémy Simard

Content Consultant:
Anthony J. Weinhaus, PhD
Assistant Professor of Integrative Biology and Physiology
University of Minnesota

magic
wagon

visit us at www.abdopublishing.com

Published by Magic Wagon, a division of the ABDO Group, 8000 West 78th Street, Edina, Minnesota, 55439. Copyright © 2011 by Abdo Consulting Group, Inc. International copyrights reserved in all countries. All rights reserved. No part of this book may be reproduced in any form without written permission from the publisher.

Looking Glass Library™ is a trademark and logo of Magic Wagon.

Printed in the United States of America, North Mankato, Minnesota.
022010
092010

 THIS BOOK CONTAINS AT LEAST 10% RECYCLED MATERIALS.

Text by Rena Korb
Illustrations by Rémy Simard
Edited by Holly Saari
Interior layout and design by Emily Love
Cover design by Emily Love

Library of Congress Cataloging-in-Publication Data
Korb, Rena B.
  My spine / by Rena Korb ; illustrated by Remy Simard ; content consultant, Anthony J. Weinhaus.
     p. cm. — (My body)
  Includes index.
  ISBN 978-1-60270-809-9
  1. Spine—Juvenile literature. I. Simard, Rémy, ill. II. Weinhaus, Anthony J. III. Title.
  RD768.K663 2011
  612.7'5—dc22
                        2009048329

Table of Contents

My Spine

Hi! I'm Amelia. I want to tell you about my spine. It helps me do many things. But what is a spine? Let's find out!

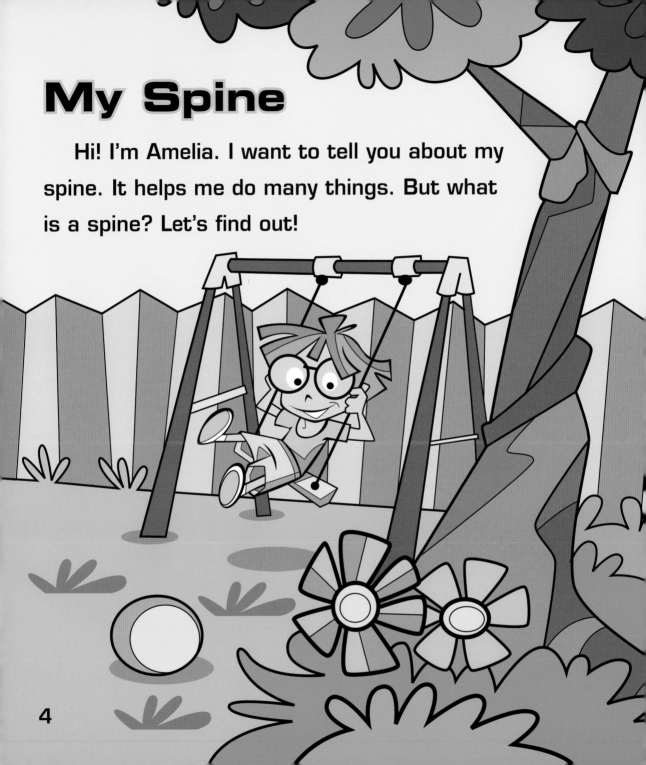

My spine is part of my skeleton. It begins at the base of my skull and goes down my back.

my spine

BACKBONE

SPINAL COLUMN

The spine is also known as the backbone or spinal column.

My spine is made up of about 30 bones.
They are connected to each other.

There are about 40,000 kinds
of animals with spines. These
include dogs and cats.

The bones of the spine are called vertebrae. Each is shaped like a ring. The vertebrae make bumps along my back and neck.

A single bone is called a vertebra. More than one are called vertebrae.

vertebrae

9

My spine has a very important job. It keeps my spinal cord safe. My spinal cord carries my brain's messages. My brain tells my body what to do.

A message goes from the brain down the spinal cord.
Then nerves carry it where it needs to go.

spinal cord

11

My spine helps me sit and stand up straight. But my spine is not straight. From the side, it looks curved like the letter *S*.

People who do not sit up straight have bad posture. This can give them pain in their necks and backs.

My spine is bendy. I can curl into a ball and touch my toes.

Sometimes a person's spine grows crooked. He or she may need to wear a back brace or have surgery to fix it.

14

Why can my spine move so easily? It is like beads on a string. Each bead, or vertebra, can move only a little bit. But the whole string, or spine, can move around a lot.

Snakes have more vertebrae than any other animal.

My spine is not just made up of vertebrae. Small disks are in between the bones. They are hard on the outside and squishy on the inside.

There are more than 1 million known animals without spines. These spineless animals include insects, snails, jellyfish, worms, and sharks.

disks

19

I jump down off my chair. The disks keep my vertebrae from rubbing against each other.

The disks are similar to your tennis shoes that cushion your feet.

21

My spine is made up of five parts. Each has its own job. The part in my neck helps keep my head up. It lets me shake my head, too.

The five parts of the spine are:
• neck (cervical)
• chest (thoracic)
• lower back (lumbar)
• hip area (sacrum)
• tailbone (coccyx)
The vertebrae in the neck are smaller and lighter than the others.

The part in my chest keeps my ribs in place. The ribs form the rib cage. It protects my heart and lungs.

Muscles are also attached to the spine. The spine helps keep them in place, too.

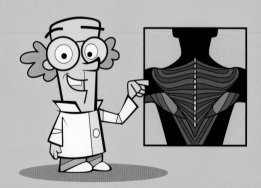

rib cage

25

My lower back carries most of my body's weight. It helps me keep my balance. The vertebrae in this part are the largest and strongest.

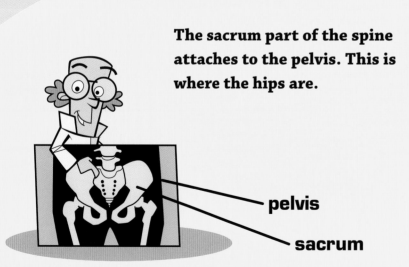

The sacrum part of the spine attaches to the pelvis. This is where the hips are.

pelvis

sacrum

My spine helps keep me safe and moving easily every day!

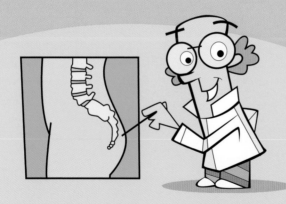

The bottom of the spine has a curved bone.
It is called the tailbone, or coccyx.

A Look Inside

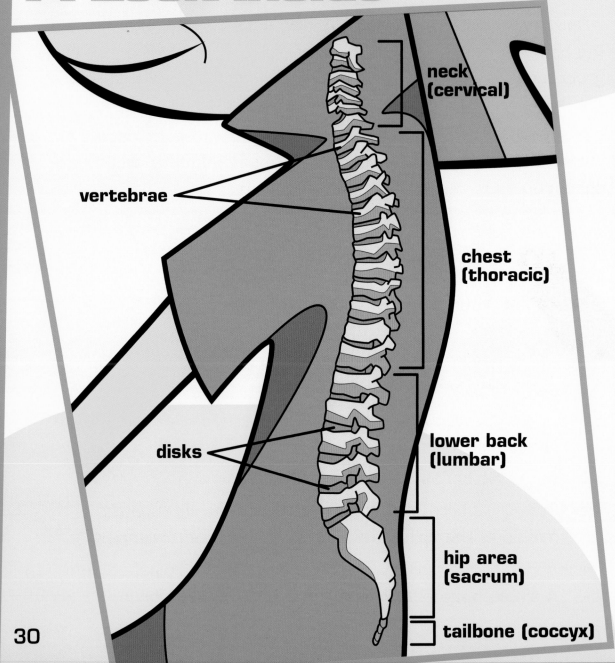

vertebrae

neck
(cervical)

chest
(thoracic)

lower back
(lumbar)

disks

hip area
(sacrum)

tailbone (coccyx)

Fun Facts

• Children have 33 vertebrae. Adults have 33, too. But some of the bones have grown together. Five vertebrae in the lower spine grow together to form the sacrum. Four more grow together at the bottom of the spine to form the coccyx.

• A newborn baby's spine is much straighter than an adult's spine. Once the baby can hold up its head and move around, its spine curves to make the normal *S* shape.

Glossary

disk – a flat, round, cushiony body part that is found between vertebrae.

nerves – clusters of cells that the body uses to send messages to and from the brain.

pelvis – the strong, bowl-shaped ring of bones near the bottom of the spine.

skeleton – the bones inside the body.

spinal cord – a cord of nerve tissue that runs through the middle of the spine and carries the brain's messages.

vertebrae (VUHR-tuh-bray) – the bones of the spinal column. A single bone is called a vertebra (VUHR-tuh-bruh).

On the Web

To learn more about the spine, visit ABDO Group online at
www.abdopublishing.com. Web sites about the spine are
featured on our Book Links page. These links are routinely
monitored and updated to provide the most current information
available.

Index